Mary's Musings

A Book of Poetry

Mary E. Reid

Made with ❤ on the BookLeaf Publishing Platform
www.bookleafpub.in
www.bookleafpub.com

Dedication

This book of poems is dedicated to the Creative community who has allowed me to try out my creativity without judgement.

Preface

In 2021 my mother passed away. My dad had been gone for more than 30 years. I felt untethered and not connected to anything any longer. As a way to work thru my grief, and becoming close friends with a creative, I decided to find my creative side. In 2023 I started going to an Open Mic with a fantastic group of people and took the risk to write some poems. These are some of the poems that I have written in the past year.

Acknowledgements

Thank you, Curtis, Mo, Jessica, October Self Care, Bruce, Demontre, Unc (Norman), Tori, Sol, Nancy, Kimberly, Zeda Stew. I want to be like you as I grow and continue to find my creative self!

Dear Daughter

Dear Daughter,
Come near and sit cause I got something to say
I know I not really yo mama but I see Young black girls
as my daughters in this day
I've lived 6 decades to your 1, 2 or three
So I feel I have some roots that are planted like a tree
From this place where I sit
I want to share with you some shit   (or share with you
a bit)
I hope yo real mom has been good to you but maybe she
aint
I am here to bring you some wisdom that maybe she
can't
No matter what she told you, you are beautiful you see
And you too will grow to be strong just like the tree
But what if you don't feel like being so strong?
That is ok too, being soft, weak or tired is never wrong
Find someone to talk to, don't keep inside
No matter how you are feeling you may have to swallow
you pride
Let others in but take some precaution
Tell the wrong ones and find their kindness was not a
good option
You body is yours, no one else can use it

Make sure it is something you want to give away and
that you are ready to lose it
Take time to know what do you like,
Are you a creative, do you like math, or do you really
like to hike?
There are so many things you are going to experience
that I can't even begin to tell you them all
One thing I know is that you may well fall
Just get back up and try again
Life is a journey with many twists
There will be highs, there will be lows, too many to list
But daughter don't let that stop you from living your life
I gotta go baby girl don't want to cause you no strife
Listening to an old woman ain't really no fun
But sometimes its just something that has to be done
I love you, will be praying for you and you take care!
And just remember I'm out here watching you, so be
aware.
Love, TiTi Mary

Couch surfing

Had to sleep on the couch tonight
cause I had nowhere to go
Worst thing is I didn't want anyone to know

My home is goes
the money is too.
I'm really not sure
what I'm going to do

Feeling alone, desperate,
I'm getting kind of cold
and really want to hide.
Cause the couch I am sleeping on
is outside.

Long and slow

He had exhausted himself
Because he had worked long
and was taking it slow
It felt so good to feel something grow
She was so excited
she thought she would explode
Her body felt so alive
She was ready to take the next dive

They wrestled and tossed
And had to rip some things off
Sometimes they sat in silence
Other times talking their thoughts aloud

They had to come to terms
With things they didn't know
Trying to find new pleasures
That could only come from going
real slow

New truths were discovered
The transformation
was a beautiful Revelation
Him or her

doesn't matter which one you be knowing
Because this is the journey of healing and growing
And it is often
Long and slow

Love

Have you ever been loved by someone just for the sake
of being loved?
No agenda, no strings attached
Just some good conversation
A good meal
Extended gazes
A slight nod for the go ahead
A touch that lingers
A full body massage
A kiss
More conversation
Some laughter
No strings attached
No future plans
Just two people exploring each other
In this moment
For this time
Making love
The comfortableness of the pleasure
No more words need to be spoken
The feeling of completeness in the universe
Your whole body is alive and humming
All is well, all stress is gone
Lying there in their arms

Hearts beating together
Falling into a peaceful sleep
No one knows what tomorrow holds
But for today, right now
Love is here
And that is enough
Have you ever been loved by someone just for the sake
of being loved

Woman Healer

If she lets you in, you will heal her soul
Listening to her talk for hours about all sorts of things
Making her laugh
Touching her in places she thought were dead
Judgement free because you aren't trying to control her
Enjoying seeing the girl in her while loving the woman
she is
You are a woman healer allowing her soul to be healed, if
she will let you.

If she lets you in, you will heal her soul
Taking the weight of mothering from her for awhile
Allowing her to get all her anger out without finding her
aggressive
Loving her messiness
Telling her about the beauty you see within her
You are a woman healer allowing her soul to be healed, if
she will let you.

If she lets you in, you will heal her soul
Letting your love cover her completely
Stroking her hair so sweetly
Holding her tightly to your chest

Reminding her that she is fearfully and wonderfully made
You are a woman healer allowing her soul to be healed, if she will let you.

Stairway to heaven

Slow and easy she said.
please go slow and easy
So he started with just gazing at her
Taking her all in
Her mounds and curves
Her aged beauty revealing itself
Then he kissed her neck
Behind the ear
Moving to her Lips.
Slow and easy
Sucking each lip,
finding her juicy tongue
Anticipating other wet places on her
but staying right here a little longer
Her neck
Smelling sweet and fragrant, arched up to receive his
kisses
He gazes at her again,
her eyes are closed
Where is she? he wonders
He moves to her chest
Mounds of fatty tissue that moves like silly putty in his
hand
His Tongue circles the nipple and they come alive.

Hard
Did she just groan?
He stays here longer - she had said slow and easy
Her back arched up
He holds her tight
His tongue goes down her stomach
And while he is going down,
He knows
He is on the stairway to heaven
Finds her spot and knows it
because she shakes
He looks up at her
she is moaning with
Her eyes still closed
but the smile
On her face....
Priceless
He goes back in, using his tongue
He feels her legs release wide open
The g spot is out,
is she trying to say something?
He slows down
Tasting her
Feeling her getting engorged
And then she explodes
He enters
Slow and easy

Moving in and out
Becoming one
All things of this world fade away as
Step by step they climb the stairway to heaven together
slow and easy
MER

Daddy's hands

I loved my daddy's hands.
I used to hold them in mine and rub my fingers over the
veins pulsing with his blood.
They were soft and
They were weathered and
They were strong
Sometimes they were grimy and had dirt in the
fingernails.
But they always showed me love.
He used his words and his hands to show me how to
transplant a plant from a pot to the ground
"Take care of the roots because they are connected to the
leaves on top"
"Dig a hole big enough to put the new plant in then fill it
with some good dirt and give it water"
He took his time and I see now how he did the very
same thing with me
He took care of my roots and provided a hole big enough
for me to grow
I feel his heartbeat in my life now because he took time
to water me, give me sunlight and nurtured me as I grew
So now when I put my hands in the earth
I am reminded that everything that happens in the world
can grow

if we take care of the roots,
give it some water
and some sun
and some space to grow
When my hands are in the dirt,
I feel connected to the heartbeat of the universe...
and I remember my Daddy.

The Loudest Voice in my Head

"It doesn't matter if you break the agreement with
yourself"
"You can try again tomorrow"
"They don't really care about you"
"You are really getting fat, old"
"You'll always be alone"
These are not very nice things to be said
 but these are the voices that are in my head

They try to rule and reign
But I'm trying to make my triumph not be in vein
Every day I have to say
I am enough, Get out of my way
I've got things to do
And in my head there is no place for you

Thoughts are just puffs of smoke
That try to make me choke
But I refuse to die because I have places to go
Leaving them alone will help me grow
I will turn to the Word that is tried and true
And God will continue showing me what do.

Cravings

What do you crave?
Food, money, sex, a drug
Does it take over your mind?
Can't think of anything else
Can't breathe
Think you will die if you don't have it
Heart racing
Breathing fast
I gotta have it
It will be so good, so satisfying
It will make me feel better
Feel loved, feel important, feel wanted, chilled out
But will it?

Satisfying a craving only leaves you feeling sad,
Defeated, wanting even more

Satisfying a food craving won't get you to your goal
While you think it will make you whole

Satisfying a craving for sex in the wrong places
Could get you all kinds of diseases
Or maybe a little baby

Satisfying a craving for money could leave you broke
Or it can make you have a stroke

The satisfaction from the drug is fleeting
And it will have you setting up another meeting

Then the craving is running you
It becomes your friend,
you check in with it,
 you always trying to satisfy it

We were made to crave by the Creator
To crave his love, his mercy, his grace
To seek his face
Strive to fulfill God's craving all your life
And you will get rid of all your strife.

I am Black History

Yes I am black History
No i haven't invented anything and I'm not famous but
Just being alive
I am part of the mystery of this thing called history.
I've sat where our ancestors could not
I am the little black girl that has been able to hold the
hand of a little white girl
I have been judged not by the color of my skin but by the
content of my character
I am black history because I defied the odds of single
motherhood raising a black male child to adulthood
I am black history because I am a product of
desegregation
I am black history even tho my people say I talk white
I am black history because I am my father's daughter, my
mother child
I am Black History because I have managed to live 6
decades
Seeing the civil right movement, and a black President
I am black history because I am resilient, I am a survivor
I am black history

The Art

An actor acts
a writer writes
A singer sings
They are all artists
An idea begins to germinate and turn into something
that they create
The piece of art is born,
The veil it torn
The artist feeds it with their blood, sweat and tears.
The art grows and evolves,
The artist may leave it alone for a while
But comes back to it for refinement
The artist might even wrestle with the piece to be sure it
is in alignment
But finally has to release it to the world
So the art can grow
Touch people,
Make an impact in the Universe
I am a mom
And my son is my piece of art.

My tribute to Spoken Word Artists and Poets

I don't spit the lines the way the spoken word artist do
Taking words making them twist and wind
Like information turned in formation
Or intention making think you in tension
Drawing pictures with words about issues that are hard
to grasp
Making the listener stop and think
Exposing revelations to different kinds of stink
So colorful and different is each poets' style
The time spent listening is always worth while

I don't spit the lines the way that some poets do
It's definitely a craft
It takes hella practice to get to that final draft
The syncopation brings attention and appreciation of the
cognition necessary for the accomplishment of the
statement that is brought forth from their soul
This is my tribute to you - those that shout the words
that yearn to be heard
Give light to pain
personify your brokenness, your love, your dreams

I don't spit the lines the way that some poets do

Your originality delights me
May God continue to allow your innovativeness to rise
Rise like a phoenix and fly
I am here paying attention
and awaiting your next creation.

Ratatouille

You have got to taste my ratatouille
It is soooo good!

I chopped up disappointment and fear
I pulled away dead layers of my heart
I sliced up all old misconceptions
Then I sautéed those old things
 in new thoughts and new mindsets
I sprinkled it with words from God

You are enough
You are loved
You are fearful and wonderfully made

Then I stirred and cooked them
so they could blend together
Of course I added a little salt for flavor

Now the dish is ready to be consumed
Brimming with flavors, a new creation

You have got to taste my Ratatouille!

Hope Less

Did you know that when you Hope Less
your world starts to look bleak
Hoping less makes you lose your direction
Being Hopeless sends you down the rabbit hole of
despair
Being hopeless stops you from setting goals
It slows you from moving forward

Hope is a muscle that has to be worked
You have to look deep inside yourself to find hope
What does it feel like?
Moving forward, ever seeking what is up ahead
Wondering about the future

Hoping more builds on itself, rising up like a mountain
Hoping more fills you up so you begin to see a future
It helps you to see the Light to get you thru the tunnel
The world because becomes brighter and bigger
Hopeful helps You to believe things will happen
Hopeful brings dreams
Hopeful gives you direction
so
Hope More

If I were a Poem

If I were a poem I would flow
from my head to my toe,
Full of words that make you think,
that soothe or heal or make you grow.

I would be a sonnet
Full of love overflowing
 Maybe sprinkled with prayers
So that you will know that God still cares.

I would be full of descriptions
Painting pictures in your mind like
Stunning rainbows, crisp cool air
Buttery soft pillows, or a wild brown bear

I'd be a eulogy,
sad and slow
To help you remember
a loss from long long ago

Then a limerick, I like to be
To make you laugh and
Find new joy on your behalf

If I were a poem,
I'd want to be
The thing you keep close to your heart
So we would never be apart.

Goddess Moon

Goddess moon
Shining bright
Bath me in your midnight light
Show me what I need to know
Direct me where I need to go
Open up my senses wide
Help me find my creative side
Heal me with your loving glow
Guide me gently because I want to grow
Then slowly put me down to sleep
So all your lessons can settle in deep
And when I awake with the rising sun
You will know your journey is done.

Peaceful Grief

Peaceful easy feeling
The moon is shining bright
The air is cool
The fire is crackling
The night sounds are happening
The frogs ribbiting
The crickets singing
A bird chirping here and there
A rustle of the grass, is that a shadow of a deer?
Thoughts of those we have lost cross your mind
And you cry and smile at the same time
You ponder about the past
Wonder about the future and
Feel satisfied with the present
You thank God for all you have been through
To get this this moment
Restful
Full of possibility
Full of hope and dreams.
A peaceful easy feeling

To My Unborn Child

Poor unborn child, beginning to grow, inside your momma you'll never know Lyrics by Seals & Crofts, Unborn Child Album

To my unborn child
In response to Demontre Lewis' poem
Many teardrops

At 19 we were young and scared
We were in college you see
And being pregnant wasn't an option for me
neither of us could think of a way to tell our parents
So we made a decision and we both agreed
He paid for it
And is probably still paying today
It's not a thing that just goes away

I haven't thought of your for quite some time,
You, the unborn child of mine
Who would you have been a daughter or son
What life did I stop that will never become
I still remember the day that they scraped you away
Curled up in a ball was I for the rest of that day

Yes it is an option, a choice and
I believe in that right
But the next time I laid down at night
and woke up with child
I had you on my mind and
There was a different resolution.

Daddy, I took you for Granted

I took you for granted, I thought you'd always be around
So when you left this world, it knocked me to the ground
Your smile lit up a room, your laugh was so hearty
One of your biggest dreams was that me and my sisters
would be smarties
Family was so important to you, it showed by how you
provided
You may not always agreed with mommy but you two
were never divided
People who knew you talk of your goodness, and being
around you was always a plus
You always helped others without any fuss.

I took you for granted, thought you'd always be around,
That you would be home when me and your grandson
came to town
You loved me so fiercely, I went confidently into the
world and found my own place
Never thinking there would be a day that I wouldn't be
able to touch your face.
I followed your footsteps in the work that I do
But not a day goes by when I wish I couldn't talk with
you.

I bought a nice house and because you were a
handyman, your spirt guides me through
Whenever there is any fixing to do.

I took you for granted, I thought you'd always be
around.
I love you and miss you daddy I now say to the ground.
But one thing your love has taught me to know
Is that love from the Lord will continue to grow
Because of this fact, I am never alone
And I know that I'll see you again at Jesus' throne.
I took you for granted and I'm sad, that is true
But the joy of the Lord helps me to get thru.
Love you Daddy!

What do I call you?

What should I call you?
We have known each other half our lives
We have slept with each other too many times to count
We've spent endless hours on the phone
But we have never shared a meal together
We haven't gone grocery shopping,
Or taken a trip or spent a whole day together
We haven't met each other friends
(oh I have talked to one of your friends once or twice
cause you wanted me to give them some advice)
Do those otherwise close to you know who I am?
My family doesn't know who you are
So what do I call you - Friend, lover, acquaintance?
I have never called you to help me out when I needed
help
You only call me when your "head" hurts
Am I your muse, do you want anything more than just
sex
What do I call you?
You who makes me feel safe when we are in each other's
arms
Your heartbeat soothes me
When you are inside me I feel as if we are one
... But here is the rub

Our communication is guarded
You don't want to say what I want to hear
I don't say and do what you want me to do the way you
want me to do it
So we play this guessing game to figure out what we are
really saying to each other
Is it time to say goodbye or at least relax expectations?
I hate going round and round with you
I don't want to never feel your heartbeat again or feel
you inside me but that is not all I want
And if that is all you can give then I will have to
sacrifice.
Because until I know what to call you
I can't move on, you can't move on
We both deserve better, we deserve the best of each
other that we can give
If we can't get there, then we need to depart which will
really break my heart.
So now it is in your hands as I have shared my thoughts,
What should I call you? What do you call me?

History

I don't talk about it often
But don't let this smile fool you
I've been through some stuff
I loved a boy and as things happen
A baby was created
and because
We were scared and
 didn't want to
Tell
We may go to hell
We took the easy way out
It's a decision I still think about
I've been thru some stuff
Don't let the smile fool ya
With that boy I tried marriage,
but he didn't understand,
his hands were not supposed to be around my neck and
No I don't Have to go with you
Oh I've been thru some stuff
Don't let this smile fool you
I have met the day that I didn't
Want to be here
I have been a Single parent
With bills that couldn't get paid

Mommy and daddy now both gone
Grief lives with me everyday
So, I have been thorough my stuff
But this smile is my stance
Because the one who has carried Me
brings me such joy
That this smile
 is His gift to you

9 789363 309494